" DO NOT FEAR MISTAKES. THERE ARE NONE."

— MILES DAVIS

Davis valued improvisation so much that he paid
his saxophonist not to practice solos at home,
"so as to avoid the polish."

STEP

02

SECOND STEP

OBSERVE

44 – 65

STEP

03

THIRD STEP

IMAGINE

66 – 83

STEP

06

SIXTH STEP

LEARN

124 – 143

STEP

07

SEVENTH STEP

ACT

144 – 161

INTRO

We're calling this Innovators Anonymous because innovation is trickier than many make it out to be; "Fail better" has become a catchphrase, but not a reality anyone wants to face. What we've found is that part of innovation is educating others about the process—during the process— so as to help them navigate the inherent twists and turns. Just as other groups provide support, we're here with our own multistep process to create a product while maintaining peace of mind.

What is that process? A way to intertwine the foundations of a solid business plan with the mechanics of creating a digital product—because what is one without the other? If there's no revenue, everything comes to a halt. If there's no process, there's no path.

By going "lean" long before it became a movement, we developed a cohesive model that has helped our clients and will hopefully help you, too. We were inspired by the structure of Eric Ries's "Build-Measure-Learn" feedback loop and decided to build upon it with a hands-on, seven-step process that speaks to everyone who seeks to innovate.

We think in diagrams, which is how we arrived at these conveyor belts in parallel on the following page, with one belt representing business, and the other, product. As the product, in this case a cake, is created, it goes through various iterations in response to consumer feedback. At the same time as it's being developed, the business is under development, too.

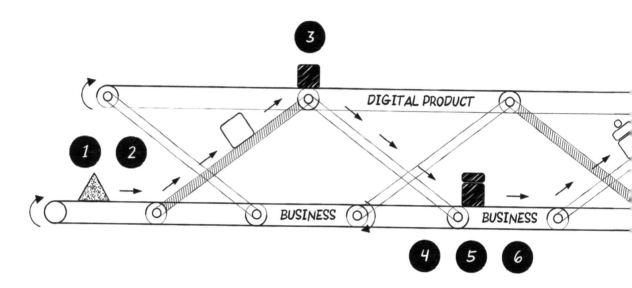

FIGURE 8. 1: BUSINESS MEETS PRODUCT

Business and product working in tandem:

1. Create new concept / steal market share (with imaginary cake business)
2. Create unique value proposition
3. Develop online commerce
4. Business process to freeze cakes and deliver by drone in 30 minutes
5. Financial model and projections
6. Facebook-targeted acquisition strategy
7. End-user feedback: Product concepts and MVP are too bland
8. Competitive analysis improves batter flavor and texture
9. End-user feedback: Too sweet
10. Product roadmap planning: Add fruit
11. Perfect! User demand seems promising, especially immediate delivery via drone

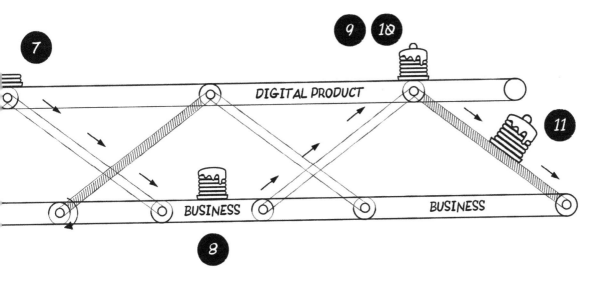

As we see it, the digital and business worlds are tied together. If you aren't clear on the value proposition, how will you know your priorities when it's time to build the product? And what use is a product without customers? Following these steps will enable you to spend money effectively; with iterative releases, you can ensure that you're delighting the customer before you invest in a highly scalable back office.

Every iteration should be fueled by data, and the questions you ask in order to get that data should be driven by the business folks and the development team. Is this venture sustainable? Are you building something people want?

We're here to help you get to yes.

The fact is that business is always messier than anyone wants to admit. But if we agree on process, the customers will show us the way.

ABOUT US

■

"Who are you, anyway?" That's what we thought when we were thrown together to help a product that wasn't finding its way. After a few days of wondering how in the world we were going to collaborate, we realized we worked together so well.

We're both into details as well as the big picture. Okay, fine, we are diagram-obsessed (don't judge!). That's how we understand the world—by mapping it out.

Side note: waking up at 4 am, getting to Penn Station before dawn, spending the day in DC, and arriving back in New York at 10:30 pm is the ultimate compatibility test. If you still like working alongside each other after that, you've found your person.

Honestly, it was a lucky break. We're really curious people, and we're always trying to figure things out as if the world were a game. We ended up seeing how good we were at distilling complex ideas and looking at a product from top to bottom and bottom-up. Whatever we did, it was so much better when we did it together.

JEANNETTE MCCLENNAN

Growing up in New York, Jeannette was a dancer at the Eglevsky Ballet School and also the only girl in her school's robotics club. "I liked creating things, and I wanted to know how they worked," she explains. Hence the move to start-ups, where the challenge of making products succeed keeps life interesting.

Jeannette—a digital technology executive who has held C-level positions at five companies—has spent her career defining and developing innovative digital products and services essential to revenue attainment and business growth. She led sales and marketing at MapQuest, which became a leader in travel and destination planning; transformed Reuters into a strategic partner able to support the creation of the Fox News Network; established Organic as an e-commerce leader delivering excellence in shopping experiences for Tommy Hilfiger, Zagat, Microsoft/Corbis, Sting/Compaq, and Garnet Hill; transformed Ogilvy Interactive's competencies to serve IBM, American Express and others as Ogilvy's first digital marketing president in North America; built Local Matters into a local search leader; spearheaded Daily Makeover's breakthrough in facial recognition "try-on" technology; and developed Life Reimagined for AARP to help people manage life transitions. She's currently delivering product and marketing strategy for Holiday Retirement's newly minted start-up, Milo.

FLAVIO MASSON

Inspired by the film *War Games*, Flavio enrolled in BASIC programming lessons at an early age. When he got his first computer, a Commodore 64, he used BASIC to create mini artificial intelligence applications that allowed him to have conversations with his computer. He went on to create multiple storylines and teach his computer to sound human.

In 2003, Flavio founded 10012, a NYC-based digital innovation firm that aligns marketing and product, keeping them in lockstop at the speed of agile. As the leader of 10012, Flavio extended Nike's indoor soccer shoe launch into four international markets; increased viewership and online engagement for Bravo TV (Project Runway) and HBO (Sleeper Cell, Elizabeth I); heightened awareness of Chase Bank in Spanish-speaking markets; and collaborated with AARP on special projects and innovation for 14 years, during which he built the largest archive of civil rights stories in the world, now housed at the Library of Congress. Currently, Flavio is employing his team at 10012 to execute the product and marketing strategy for Milo. Flavio is also the founder/CEO of Rangri.com.br, a Brazil-based for-profit food ordering platform with a social mission at its core: order food, end hunger.

WHY A BOOK?

■

Because we have a way of working that we wanted to share. We codified it, customized it, and we believe in it as a better method of dealing with the challenges to disruption. It's designed for all the uncertainty you'll face, so that you're not constantly losing your mind as you're innovating. We've spent our whole careers developing this process; we learn by doing, and we've done this for a long time. This is our way of passing along what we've learned.

HOW TO READ IT

The following pages will help you to confront the barriers to creating something that doesn't already exist—and trying to sell it. The seven steps won't push you toward a particular outcome; they're an outline of the process for you to follow.

How might a process help? No matter where your business is in the maturation process, it's hard to face the flaws in your assumptions and hypotheses, and this is a way to face those flaws. No one wants to find out that the first attempts to meet their needs are wrong, but if you're open to challenging your own assumptions, and you want to listen and learn, this is the perfect book for you.

As you'll see, each step operates from a different mind-set: while in Assess we advise openness, once you get to Act it's time to be decisive. Every chapter is broken up into subsections and figures galore (we warned you!). At the end of each step, we highlight the key takeaways as an easy reference tool. Speaking of which, we think of this as a workbook to return to time and again. We hope you will, too.

ASSESS

EXAMINE
YOUR GOALS

STEP

01

TIP THE SCALE IN YOUR FAVOR

Everyone knows it's difficult to articulate business goals. That's why we can't give you the answers. But we can ask the right questions so you can find your own answers. A great starting point is to consider the size of your business opportunity by turning your gaze inwards, or, as we like to say, using an internal lens. Take everything you know and don't know about your business—market size, competitive landscape, consumer-adoption trends, your company's innate strengths, operational capabilities, technology patents—to create scenarios of what the future might look like. You can think of these scenarios as counterweights that minimize the risk related to unknowns, thereby tipping things in your favor. We call this exercise **"Tip the Scale."** Just remember: if you're creating something new, don't let your prior experiences cloud your judgment.

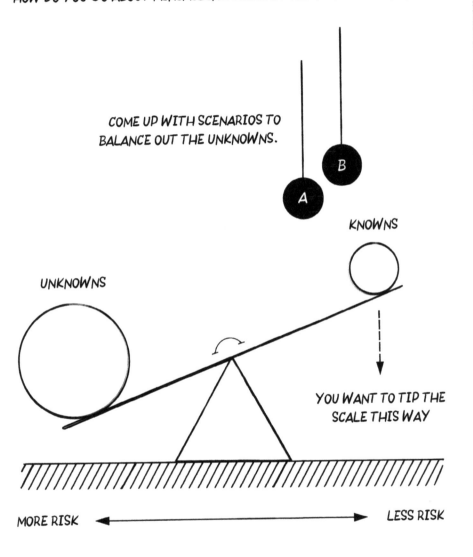

FIGURE 1. 1: TIP THE SCALE
HOW DO YOU GO ABOUT MINIMIZING RISK? BY REDUCING THE UNKNOWNS.

COME UP WITH SCENARIOS TO
BALANCE OUT THE UNKNOWNS.

KNOWNS

UNKNOWNS

YOU WANT TO TIP THE
SCALE THIS WAY

MORE RISK ⟷ LESS RISK

START WITH AN INTERNAL HYPOTHESIS ABOUT WHAT WILL BENEFIT YOUR BUSINESS.

BE UP-FRONT

Passion for your idea is what fuels this entire process. If you can convince yourself—through empirical data—of the value of this opportunity, go ahead and engage your colleagues in a healthy debate. In our experience, contrasting views are good for business, and others may appreciate an open, honest exchange.

START SMALL

Believe it or not, the smaller the team, the better, because your business needs will evolve over time. This evolution—an unpredictable journey into learning what your consumers want—will require that your team not only be talented, but also have the ability to adapt. Many people are incredibly skilled but can't handle that kind of uncertainty, as it can be unsettling. But if the research shows that you need to pivot, you need everyone on your team to pivot with you.

You also want to look at the team dynamic. Have these people worked well together in the past? If they're new to each other, arrange meet-ups so you can see how everyone will interact. If one person out of four doesn't get along with the rest, it will weaken the collaborative spirit.

Finally, stay on top of what everyone is doing. When contemplating whether or not to make a hire, consider: Does this job description meet the most immediate needs of the business? You need to ask yourself: Is everyone being utilized at 150 percent? This is an important question, though not because you want to overwork anyone. It's simply that the smaller the team, the stronger the partnership. And once you're ready to grow, you will make those new hires. By then you'll know that they're necessary.

DON'T BUILD THE TAJ MAHAL JUST YET. **START TINY** SO THAT YOU CAN MAP THE OPPORTUNITY IN A MANAGEABLE WAY AND GO FROM THERE.

ALL ABOUT

SPRINTS

We recommend an agile approach to speed up progress. Not familiar with the term "sprint"? (Don't sweat it.) It's a boxed cycle your team will depend on for planning and execution, and it typically lasts one to four weeks. Some teams work better with rapid timelines, but there is nothing wrong with choosing to work in three- or four-week cycles. Any longer than four weeks and you have "waterfall" development, a more linear approach where everything is done in sequence, making it harder to pivot quickly and efficiently. See if you can apply the sprint cycle across the entire business (even for tasks that don't fall under development), so everyone is working at the same pace. As you'll see in the following diagram, in an agile approach many functions work in parallel, making pivots easier to implement.

FIGURE 1. 2: AGILE VERSUS WATERFALL DEVELOPMENT

AGILE INCORPORATES BITE-SIZED LEARNINGS INTO EACH DEVELOPMENT SPRINT,
WHEREAS ONE LEARNING INFORMS THE WATERFALL PROCESS.

AGILE

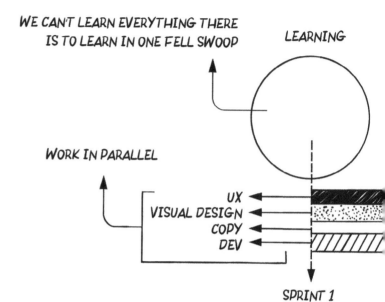

WATERFALL

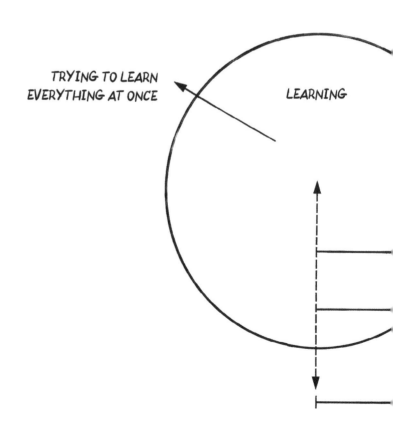

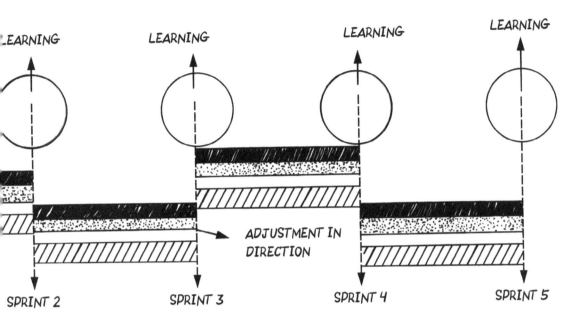

LEARNING   LEARNING   LEARNING   LEARNING

ADJUSTMENT IN
DIRECTION

SPRINT 2   SPRINT 3   SPRINT 4   SPRINT 5

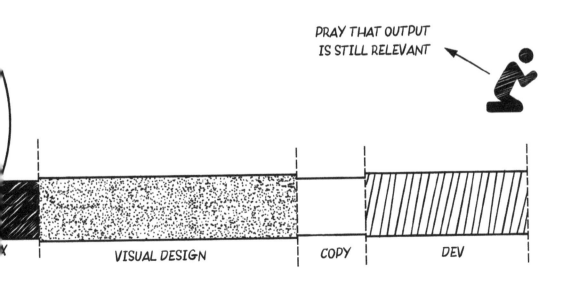

PRAY THAT OUTPUT
IS STILL RELEVANT

VISUAL DESIGN   COPY   DEV

IF YOU

DEFINE SUCCESS

As for measuring progress, what looks like a winning business opportunity to you might not appear that way to your stakeholders, which is why everyone needs to agree on the criteria for success. As you do so, watch out for feel-good metrics that don't move the needle, also known as **Vanity Metrics,** appropriately coined by Eric Ries. Vanity metrics make it look like you've met the needs of your end user, but they are actually false positives because the numbers you're looking at are not essential to the adoption and ongoing use of your product or service. Side note: Vanity metrics will keep coming into play, so be prepared to knock them down in a continual game of Whac-A-Mole. No matter the business you're in, the number of free app downloads, for instance, will often be a vanity metric. Instead, focus on whether end users are spending time on your app or making in-app purchases—those are the metrics that count.

DOING

FEEL A BIT KNOCKED OFF YOUR FEET DURING THIS PROCESS

YOU ARE IT RIGHT.

O P

MIND-SET

"BEFORE ANYTHING ELSE, PREPARATION IS THE KEY TO SUCCESS."

— ALEXANDER GRAHAM BELL

While attempting to perfect the telegraph, Bell became transfixed by something else entirely—the transmission of the human voice—no doubt inspired by having worked with the deaf alongside his father.

WEIGH YOUR PRIORITIES

While digital can be cost-efficient, don't let yourself get seduced by the notion that well-executed digital product innovation is cheap. You have to prioritize end-to-end business plan spending—what to do and when—based on the consistent removal of unknowns. For example, you wouldn't want to throw your money at a scaled system architecture before your site has traffic, and you wouldn't want to write the perfect tagline before defining your product. It's easy to fall into the trap of **Stupid Money,** but we'll help you steer clear.

Affordability should be the focus when putting together your business road map. That can be accomplished by thinking about the product first and looking for proof that the product will prevail. In a mature business, it's common sense to start with the brand and build out a communications plan, but in this case you want to **Swim Against the Tide** by starting with product. You'll also want to stay in stealth mode; this is not the time for big PR announcements. Give yourself the time to experiment while protecting your company's brand.

FIGURE 1. 3: LEARN TO SWIM AGAINST THE TIDE

START BY TRULY UNDERSTANDING YOUR PRODUCT EVEN IF IT FEELS LIKE EVERYONE ELSE WANTS
TO FOCUS ON FINISHING TOUCHES.

UNWILLINGNESS

UNKNOWNS

DEATH BY A

KNOW WHAT TO

DON'T FALL

TO SEE YOUR AND KNOWNS IS LIKE THOUSAND CUTS. WATCH FOR — AND PREY TO DENIAL.

CHECKLIST—

⊘ What is the unmet need you're trying to fill? Are you the one to meet this need? Will what you're offering require a change of behavior? Without the service or product you're creating, how does your audience currently experience the need you are trying to meet?

⊘ As you endeavor to deeply understand the unmet need, are you building and testing your value proposition?

⊘ What are your business goals? For a new line of business, what revenue stream are you targeting? If you're building on an existing revenue base, are you seeking acquisition?

⊘ How are you assessing the costs of the digital business? Have you established your long-term milestones to measure everything from the strategic value of your business to its profitability? Cost considerations: customer service, e-commerce, and digital marketing. If it's a subscription business, consider the cost of retention and the impact of churn.

◯ Is your team comprised of people with prior digital experience, also known as digital natives? How do you plan to grow your team and define your culture?

◯ Measure your **Known to Unknown** ratio: how much do you know, and how much don't you know, about this product or service you want to offer?

◯ How do your goals correlate to the user journey? State your worst and best-case scenarios then consider how your **'What Ifs'** are counterbalancing some of the unknowns.

◯ Are you organizing this new effort to give yourself the ability to let it go if you don't see the business, product, or team growing as anticipated?

01.

Look through
an internal lens

02.

Be willing to see
things as they are

03.

Accept discomfort
as part of the process

KEY
TAKEAWAYS

04.

Find the key facts
and figures to guide
decision-making

05.

Negotiate how success
will be measured
and get stakeholder
alignment

Want to see our process in action?
Visit InnovatorsAnonymous.com/Case-Studies

OBSERVE
FOLLOW
YOUR INSIGHT

STEP

02

IF YOU

LOOK OUT

Turn the lens from internal to external. Look to the outside world to discover the insights that will inform the unmet need you identified at the Assess stage. Take this opportunity to fully explore the pain point. What can be done better? Faster? Cheaper? More efficiently? **Be curious enough about your end users to discover what they need.**

COULD

DON'T PUT THE CONSUMER AT THE CENTER OF YOUR EXPERIENCE, ALL YOUR EFFORTS GO TO WASTE.

OPEN
YOUR EYES

In the early days of MapQuest, which had the largest share of online mapping services in the US (and is now second to Google Maps), the conventional wisdom was that consumers wanted to see maps of the world—but it didn't take long to learn that they wanted directions along with maps. The insight? People would rather get directions online than ask strangers for help.

What do you need to learn to get inside the end user's thought process? Should you observe them in action? Conduct real-time research? Host a focus group? Whatever you choose, your method should have these qualities: speed, flexibility (options for both quan-ti-tative and qualitative), ability to iterate, and multimedia capabilities. For instance, say you ask potential customers a question on a survey, and after you see the results you realize there is another question to ask. You should be able to formulate this new question—and ask it—in a matter of days, not weeks or months. That's why we recommend using a rapid test panel (personally, we're fans of AlphaHQ.com).

As you gather insights, be sure to compare and contrast your product concept against other players. How are competitors solving the unmet need? How does their solution compare to your own? Bring your **Knowns**, **Unknowns and What-Ifs** into the process as another evaluative tool. Fully understanding end-user behavior as well as your competitors will help you shape your vision.

KNOW THAT YOU CAN'T YOUR CONSUMER; THE COME FROM

IMPOSE
INSIGHT UPON THE
INSIGHT HAS TO
THE CONSUMER.

GET A REACTION

A cost-effective way to communicate an idea and get a fast read on it is to use stimuli, ranging from product descriptions to copy to napkin sketches to comps. By using a rapid test panel and turning your attention to qualitative and quantitative measurement, you can answer this question: how does your end user respond? Let yourself see what's really happening, not just what you want to see—because what's so powerful about truly understanding a user's likes and dislikes at this stage is that you can course-correct, which can save you a whole lot of money down the road. At this point, don't worry about branding. (In fact, branding can become a distraction if you're trying to learn something about the core idea.)

FIGURE 2. 1: START HERE
PUTTING YOUR IDEAS DOWN ON PAPER—LITERALLY—CAN BE
INCREDIBLY COST-EFFECTIVE AND ELUCIDATING. THESE SKETCHES
COME FROM THE LEAD-UP TO AN ACTUAL PRODUCT LAUNCH.

CHANCES ARE

YOU'LL GET

BEGINNING—BUT

ON THE

IT RIGHT

IT WRONG IN THE
YOU'LL BE
PATH TO GETTING
LATER ON.

WHERE'S THE WHY?

An experiment we typically run in the earlier stages of forming a product is around value proposition. Figuring out a value proposition for your product or service is a way of building a foundation that allows the product to take shape. We create a simple description of the product or service and list potential benefits to the end user as a way to rank their preferences. This exercise illuminates points of clarity, points of confusion, initial reactions, how users might describe the product or service to a friend, the likelihood of users signing up, and potentially even price.

How do you go about drafting value propositions? We're fans of Simon Sinek's "Golden Circle": Sinek suggests starting with the reason your company exists, then looking at how you go about your mission, and finally explaining what you do. Sinek believes that people don't buy what you're selling but rather why you're selling it; what you believe resonates with them, and that inspires them to make a purchase. Hence your value proposition doesn't come from the "what"—a list of features and functions— but the "why."

A TOUCH OF HUMILITY

Our best advice? Be willing to be wrong. Insight often begins in one place and ends up in another, which underlines the importance of prototyping. One challenge to discovering worthy insights is that they're often obscured by a massive pool of data. How do you cut through the noise? By creating a coherent narrative and by ensuring that your data speaks the same language. Then ask yourself again: are you satisfying the unmet need?

"WE MAY ENCOUNTER MANY DEFEATS BUT WE MUST NOT BE DEFEATED."

— MAYA ANGELOU

Best known for her autobiography *I Know Why the Caged Bird Sings,* Maya Angelou became one of the most prominent African-American writers, despite having been born in the Jim Crow South.

CU
OU

RI-
JS

CHECKLIST—

☑ What do your best customers look like? Think demographic and psychographic (personality, values, opinions, attitudes, interests, and lifestyle).

☑ Do you have a clear value proposition that you can build your business on? Or do you need to take the time to create a value proposition that stakeholders support?

☑ What behavior have you observed in your most engaged customers? Least engaged? Remember that you can learn from both.

☑ How does your target cohort currently use technology, if at all?

☑ How is your consumer currently interacting with you? List the top five methods of engagement.

☑ Can you trust your insights? Cross-check them and look for replicable results.

☑ Does your insight clearly differentiate you from your competitors? Are you replacing something that's already being done elsewhere? Is there a market for this?

☑ Is the product already on the market? What customer-service feedback do you have and how might this serve as a source of insight gathering?

☑ Is this an ancillary product? Look at the current journey of your customer in your attempt to meet this need.

01.

Look through an
external lens

02.

Define the unmet need
you want to solve for

KEY

TAKEAWAYS

03.

Gain a deep understanding
of the end user's points of
friction or dissatisfaction

———

04.

Begin to see ways to
reduce the unknowns

———

Want to see our process in action?
Visit InnovatorsAnonymous.com/Case-Studies

IMAGINE
UNLEASH YOUR
CREATIVITY

STEP

03

EXPLORE WITH LIMITS

While this is an expansive step, you're not starting from scratch —you're working with everything you discovered in Assess and Observe to frame the problem you're trying to solve. Within that frame, you have endless possibilities. Capture every idea that comes to mind.

The inherent paradox of the imagine space is that you want to support maximum possibility while staying within the established frame. You're not solving all of the world's problems; you're trying to solve one problem for a particular set of end users in a particular way. And you're not creating the product yet—you're engaged in an incredibly valuable exercise so that you know what to do once you're ready to move forward.

AT THIS POINT
YOUR PROBLEM
IS WELL DEFINED.
YOUR SOLUTION
SHOULDN'T BE—AND
THAT'S WHAT YOU'LL
BE PLAYING WITH.

AUDACIOUS

CIOUS
DACIO
AUDAC
JS AU

IT'S TIME TO
SUMMON ALL OF
YOUR CREATIVITY
TO IMAGINE HOW
YOU CAN
NEED YOU'VE

CHOOSE WISELY

Who should your stakeholders be? Consider having representation from up to five carefully selected personnel from your company. Make sure technology leadership is represented in the room—a digital product cannot thrive without deep knowledge of the latest advancements that would work for a broad range of your target audience. Be sure to include representatives from your innovation, product, and marketing teams, too.

MEET THE UNMET
DISCOVERED.

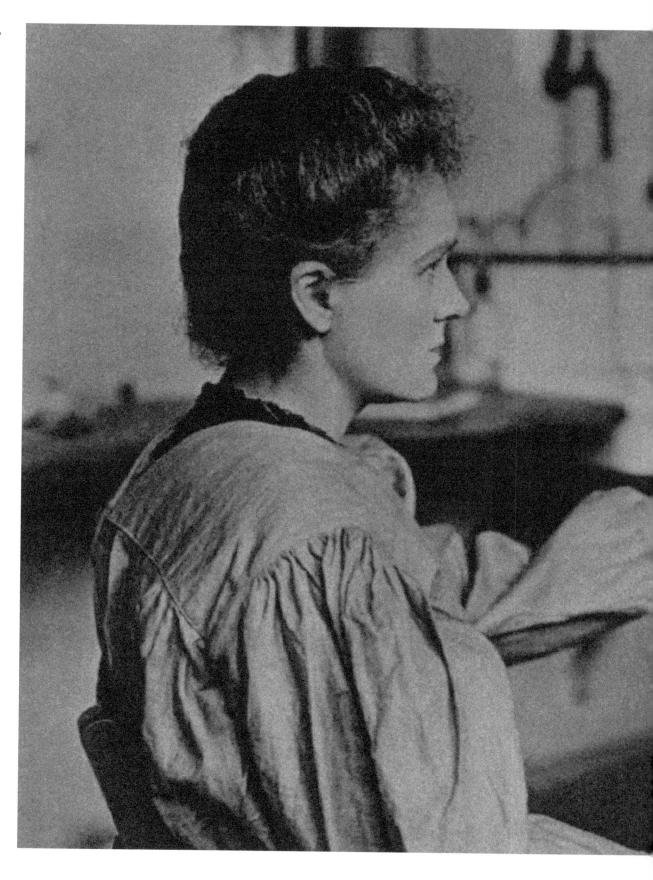

"HAVE NO FEAR OF PERFECTION, YOU'LL NEVER REACH IT."

— MARIE CURIE

Marie Curie's relentless pursuit of scientific knowledge led her from Poland to Paris, where her research on radium garnered her not one but two Nobel Prizes—the first in physics, the second in chemistry.

GET MESSY

Your initial ideation sessions should build on each other as if guided by the improvisational comedy standard *"yes, and,"* where you not only accept what's being proposed, but add to it. This creates an environment where no idea is wrong, and everyone can share freely. You should feel comfortable putting your idea out there even if you're in the minority. We're not suggesting a retelling of *The Emperor's New Clothes,* but we do think that the messiness of brainstorming drives this step at the outset. Keep in mind that the generative space should be free from interruption. Also, you'll probably need more than one session, and if you can meet out of the office, that's even better.

Remember: fear and insecurity simply cannot run the show. Instead, curiosity and courage are paramount. Be curious enough to explore each perspective and courageous enough to share something new. Equip each member of your team with information about **Knowns and Unknowns** from **Tip the Scale** as a point of reference so that you are well positioned to gather fresh insights. These should be able to help you further **Tip the Scale** in the right direction.

The aim of this step is not only the development of the ideas themselves, but also the ability to articulate their impact using **Tip the Scale.** How has the information in **Tip the Scale** been influenced by the Imagine process? What questions are you addressing and how are you further molding the product you want to bring to market?

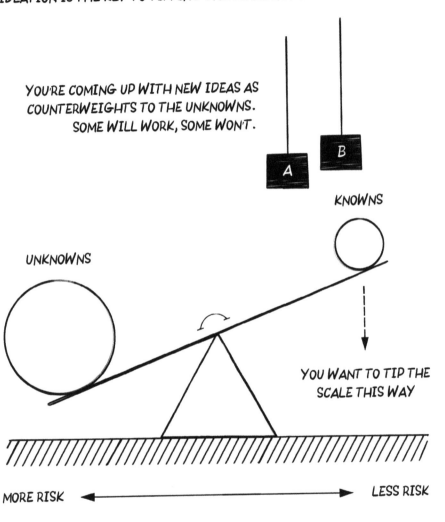

FIGURE 3. 1 : NEW IDEAS AS COUNTERWEIGHTS
IDEATION IS THE KEY TO TIPPING THE SCALE IN YOUR FAVOR.

YOU'RE COMING UP WITH NEW IDEAS AS
COUNTERWEIGHTS TO THE UNKNOWNS.
SOME WILL WORK, SOME WON'T.

A

B

KNOWNS

UNKNOWNS

YOU WANT TO TIP THE
SCALE THIS WAY

MORE RISK ⟷ LESS RISK

ULTIMATELY, INFORMATION THE DRIVING FORCE NOT CONSENSUS, NOT NOT VOTING, NOT THE NOT HIERARCHY,

SHOULD BE IN DECISION MAKING—THE DECISION OF ONE, LOUDEST VOICE, AND NOT A PILE UP.

CHECKLIST—

☑ What criteria will persuade you to move forward with an idea? List pros and cons. Be willing to examine the negatives and discard the idea if necessary. Ensure that there is real discussion. If necessary, use a strong moderator to cross-examine each concept.

☑ What would the rollout look like? How would your idea become a reality? Give yourself a breather in order to imagine each step of the process.

☑ Think in terms of episodic versus habitual consumption. What usage patterns does your product need to achieve its business metrics? Note: not all products have to be habit-forming to be successful.

☑ What's the potential for growth? Does each idea have potential for cost-effective distribution? If you are a mature business can you leverage assets for distribution channels from your existing business? How will you scale your product or service? Is scaling up an obstacle on the path to success?

Pull out your financial model. How does your Imagine work mesh with your financial assumptions from Assess? Do you need to re-frame it? Move to a subscription model from a single transactional business model? What are the implications of the cost of getting to market? Can you come up with scale and distribution alternatives? What are the implications for financial analyses such as break-even point or Return on Investment (ROI)?

How will you measure success? (Don't let **Vanity Metrics** sneak in!)

Have you compared your product to others in the marketplace? This will help you lay out hypotheses to test in future steps so you know whether success has been achieved.

01.

Be open to multiple ways
to address the internal and
external data that point
to a real market need

02.

Explore all the options
and be willing to rule out
many of them

KEY
TAKEAWAYS

03.

Visualize how each
idea would come to life

04.

Observe how new ideas
can influence **Tip the Scale**
in unexpected ways

Want to see our process in action?
Visit InnovatorsAnonymous.com/Case-Studies

CREATE
BUILD YOUR
PROTOTYPE

STEP

04

WHAT'S YOUR GUESS?

The exercise here is twofold: creating hypotheses and determining how you'll go about building user experiences. Hypotheses are educated guesses about what might happen based on limited evidence, and they build the foundation of every business. For example, when Percy Spencer learned that magnetrons trapped inside a metal box would heat up objects, his hypothesis was that people would be interested in using that breakthrough technology to heat up food. And so the microwave was born.

YOU'RE LEARNING AS YOU GO, WHICH MEANS YOU'RE BEING COST-EFFECTIVE AND MINIMIZING RISK.

MINIMIZE INVESTMENT, MAXIMIZE LEARNINGS

When it comes to building user experiences, chances are you have already created stimuli and learned from them in previous steps. At this point you're probably anxious to get going with your **Minimum Viable Product (MVP)**, the first real iteration of the product. **MVPs** tend not to be smooth, and that's okay, because you'll want to make sure your value proposition holds up before you start polishing or adding new features. **MVPs** require development unless you are able to use off-the-shelf technology solutions. Consider creating a library of reusable elements you can string together to rapidly create new user experiences. Here's a peek at some of the components of an engagement toolkit we've developed over the years. Feel free to build your own.

COMPONENTS OF OUR
ENGAGEMENT TOOL KIT

SIZE THE BUBBLES

A PINCH-AND-ZOOM TYPE ACTIVITY
THAT HELPS REVEAL USERS' RELATIVE
PRIORITIES

VISION BOARD

A VISUAL BOARD ORGANIZED BY
CATEGORIES USERS CAN POPULATE
WITH IMAGES AND TEXT

SPECTRUM

STREAMLINED EXPERIENCE FOR
GATHERING INFORMATION ON USERS'
MOOD IN REAL TIME

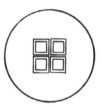

QUADRANTS

A RATING ACTIVITY THAT PRODUCES A
SCATTER PLOT OF AGGREGATE
BEHAVIORAL FEATURES

SWIPE RIGHT

A SYSTEM FOR HELPING USERS ARRIVE
AT CONCLUSIONS OF THEIR OWN

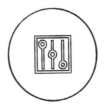

MIXER

AN INTUITIVE RATING ACTIVITY FOR
UNVEILING A COMPLETE PICTURE
OF USERS' SENTIMENTS

MOSAIC

A COLLECTION OF IMAGES AND
CONCEPTS THAT PAINT A PICTURE OF
USERS' PREFERENCES/BEHAVIOR

JOURNAL

QUESTIONS THAT ENCOURAGE USERS
TO REFLECT DEEPLY ON
PREDETERMINED TOPICS

CARD SORTING

A USER-CENTERED DESIGN METHOD
THAT PRODUCES INSIGHTS INTO USERS'
MENTAL MODELS

PROGRESS TRACKER

AN ADD-ON MODULE FOR
MEASURING START-FAIL-
COMPLETE METRICS

Before committing to your **MVP,** consider creating a prototype—a series of low- to high-fidelity "flats" that help simulate an experience without the need for code (which means you're saving money). Depending on what you're interested in learning, consider stripping your prototype of its look and feel so that users can focus on features and functions. This will eliminate distracting feedback along the lines of "I don't like this shade of green." In some cases look and feel is unavoidable because people need context, and that's what high-fidelity prototypes provide.

Should you skip prototypes? How do you decide? The bottom line is that you're here to learn—fast. Where possible, we build prototypes, as they're cheaper and faster to construct, often with no compromise in the quality of what we learn.

When creating your **MVP,** be sure to avoid building a **Very Done Viable Product (VDVP),** a ridiculous acronym we made up because it's so tempting to add bells and whistles prematurely. Save the cash for later. This might feel counterintuitive, but the focus here should be on affordability and speed. **VDVPs** are the ultimate temptress. Stay strong!

FIGURE 4. 1 : MATCH YOUR SPEND

THE AMOUNT OF MONEY INVESTED IN THE PRODUCT NEEDS TO CORRELATE
TO THE SCALE OF KNOWNS AND UNKNOWNS.

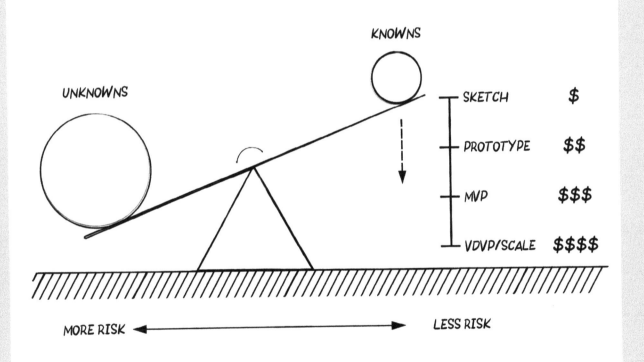

KEY WORDS: AFFORDABLE, AND

FAST,

CUSTOMER-CENTRIC.

GET IN SYNC

If you haven't done so already, this is a good time for the entire team (or, at minimum, the product team) to adopt sprint cycles. Remember: you cannot possibly learn everything there is to know about your idea all at once, and you wouldn't want to. An agile approach gives you the latitude to adapt as you go.

Have a look at all the specialists you will need to build best-in-class digital products. Some roles will be familiar, while others will pull from domains that are unique to the digital world. In addition, it goes without saying that building a common language and work style will help your team work more collaboratively. Collaboration services like Slack, Trello, Jira, and Confluence facilitate real-time communication, and provide organizational tools and access to information. If these services are new to you, you might feel overwhelmed at first, but you'll get the hang of it. (And if they're old to you, something better has probably cropped up since we published this edition. Technology, hurrah!)

FIGURE 4. 2: HOW PRODUCTS GET MADE

THE PRODUCTION LINE FOR ALL THINGS DIGITAL
TYPICALLY LOOKS LIKE THIS:

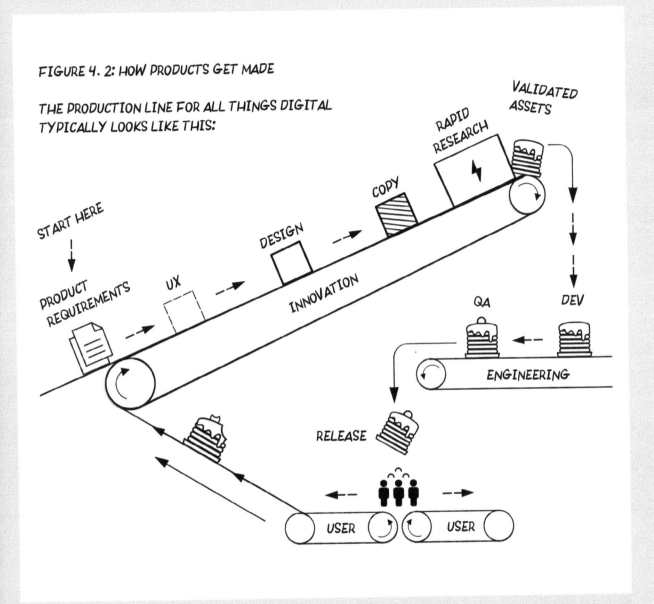

"ALL OUR DREAMS CAN COME TRUE IF WE HAVE THE COURAGE TO PURSUE THEM."

— WALT DISNEY

Disney, who began his career as an illustrator, won 22 Academy Awards—more than any other individual—for his innovation, short films, feature films, and documentaries.

INVEN

MIND–SET

CHECKLIST—

☑ Have you determined the best approach to test and learn about your product or service? Prototype or direct to MVP?

☑ Have you created a roadmap and determined the hero of each release?

☑ Have you vetted your hypotheses to make sure they are crisp and clear?

☑ Have you determined your expanded team structure and sprint cycle preferences?

Do your stimuli incorporate distracting elements that will prevent you from learning what you want to learn? For example, "I don't like that shade of green," when you're hoping to learn about features and functions.

Is your user experience addressing the unmet need? Keep coming back to this question.

Is your team aligned on the collaboration tools you're planning to use (i.e., Jira, Slack, Google Docs, Invision, etc.)?

01.

Refine insights to
move into product
prototyping

_____

02.

Find substantial evidence that the
envisioned product can leverage end-user
trends and behavior indicators to address
the unmet need

_____

KEY
TAKEAWAYS

03.

Further shape the team
and come up with a way of
working collaboratively

Want to see our process in action?
Visit InnovatorsAnonymous.com/Case-Studies

QUANTIFY

FIND YOUR METRICS

STEP

KNOW YOUR VARIABLES

You have your prototypes or MVPs from Create and you're ready to test your hypotheses in a series of experiments. As with your science project in middle school, you're listing your assumptions and finding out if you guessed right. (But this time you're not playing with your parents' money.) This will help you get answers and discover patterns, which will inform the upcoming steps in your journey—to improve your product and create the best chance for success.

What makes a hypothesis worthwhile? Its focus on a discrete, engaging interaction with an end user that can be evaluated both qualitatively and quantitatively. Basically, you need to be able to measure whether your hypothesis is correct. How will you do that? By limiting the variables, coming up with a method and a primary set of metrics. Whether you're creating a new product or enhancing an existing one, the list of unknowns is long and metrics are a way of minimizing risk. Because what's the sense in investing in a product that might struggle for adoption or simply not satisfy a need? (Psst... this is another time to watch out for **Vanity Metrics.**)

MEASURE UP

Metrics are specific to the business at hand, but we tend to use these again and again. Once you know your hypotheses, you should have a good idea of what you need to know in order to determine whether you guessed right. It's important to agree on how you'll measure progress, and, most importantly, to use the right tools.

- Willingness to Pay (WTP)
- Engagement (Daily Active User/Monthly Active User or DAU/MAU)
- Adoption Signals: Edge case vs. common (it's tied to engagement)
- Customer Acquisition Costs (CAC)
- Start-Fail/Complete (measures user progress and abandonment)
- Average Revenue Per User (ARPU)
- K-factor to measure viral growth of your audience

BEWARE OF

STATS

YOU LOOK GOOD

DON'T MAP

TO

VANITY METRICS—

THAT MAKE

BUT

BACK

INCREASED SALES.

FIGURE 5. 1: THE JOURNEY

HERE'S A SAMPLE FUNNEL FOR A TRANSACTIONAL FOOD-DELIVERY SERVICE. A FUNNEL IS THE TOTALITY OF THE USER'S EXPERIENCE WITH YOUR PRODUCT. FOLLOW THE STEPS TO SEE WHAT METRICS WOULD BE APPROPRIATE IN THIS SCENARIO.

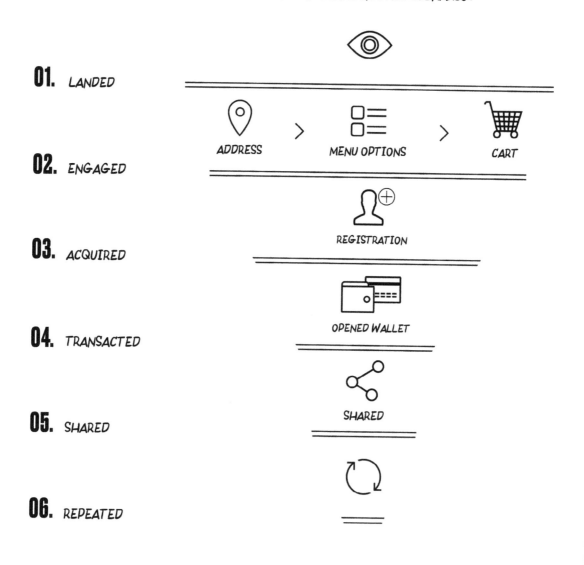

01. LANDED

ADDRESS > MENU OPTIONS > CART

02. ENGAGED

REGISTRATION

03. ACQUIRED

OPENED WALLET

04. TRANSACTED

SHARED

05. SHARED

06. REPEATED

01. This depends on sourcing the right traffic. The goal is never solely about volume of visits, but about securing visits that are most likely to deliver the action you want.

02. Actions that indicate an intent to order food, such as adding an address, searching for restaurants, browsing restaurants, or perusing menus.

03. The definition of "acquired" in this case is a user successfully completing registration, which might look like confirming their email address. Customer Acquisition Cost (CAC) is a key metric here, and you want to monitor the channels that are working best for you.

04. Finally, some "wallet action"; users have successfully transacted on the platform, thereby turning into "diners." Unfortunately, not all acquisitions lead to wallet action. Users may change their mind, get stuck due to technical glitches (uh oh!), or get distracted. Your work isn't done until the order is confirmed—and fulfilled.

05. A percentage of users will be interested in sharing their transaction, so you want your technology to facilitate that. Shared transactions help boost the the K-factor, which measures any viral growth of your customer base. These shares bring new users to the platform for no additional cost.

06. Repeat is typically measured by a relatively standard metric called DAU/MAU, or Daily Active Users over Monthly Active Users. What do we mean by active user in this case? Someone who takes an action toward ordering food (entering a delivery address, browsing restaurant menus, etc.). When you measure DAU/MAU, you'll see whether there is increasing or decreasing engagement.

"ALL RIGHT, BOYS, LET'S START HER UP AND SEE WHY SHE DOESN'T WORK."

— JOHN FRITZ

With little formal training, Fritz, an "empirical engineer," pioneered steel and iron production. He perfected the Bessemer process at what is now known as Bethlehem Steel and innovated for the US Navy.

ANALYTICAL

MIND–SET

ANALYTICAL

ANALYTICAL

MIND-SET

ANALYTICAL

CHOOSING
IS A GREAT
TO
YOUR

METRICS

OPPORTUNITY

QUESTION

TABOOS.

CHECKLIST—

⊙ Have you aligned your team around the best set of metrics to track your business end to end?

⊙ Have you set up clear and concise hypotheses to apply to your metric library?

⊙ Have you cross-checked your metrics with factors discovered in **Tip the Scale?** Metrics are counterweights for some of the unknowns you may have.

⊙ Have you conceived of your end-user funnel to guide the right traffic to the action you want?

☑ Have you screened out any vanity metrics that tried to creep in?

☑ Have you studied your competitors' funnel tactics? Are you using best practices where possible?

☑ Are you exploring the metrics that are best suited for your business? For instance, a subscription business needs to consider metrics such as Lifetime Value (LTV).

01.

Develop hypotheses to test

___

KEY

TAKEAWAYS

02.

Determine the quickest
way to learn what you
need to learn

—————

03.

Avoid vanity metrics
at all costs

—————

Want to see our process in action?
Visit InnovatorsAnonymous.com/Case-Studies

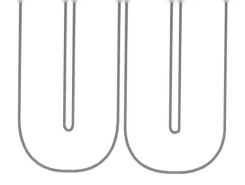

LEARN
LISTEN TO
YOUR DATA

STEP

06

GO FAST TO GO SLOW

Here's your opportunity to learn from Create and Quantify. By this point, your prototype or MVP is working from hypotheses grounded in the appropriate metrics, which lets you step back and ask yourself: What is working? What isn't working? If more testing is in order, speed is a factor here—run a sequence of rapid experiments to get the answers you need.

Once answers are in hand, slow down. Interpreting your data takes time, and its importance cannot be understated. Don't rush this. And don't worry about how long it will take to build the next prototype or MVP release; iterations should be relatively quick now that you have your assets. By now you'll be able to think of assets like building blocks that can be reconfigured with greater ease.

This is the time to come face to face with your end user's **Moments of Truth**. The **Moment of Truth** refers to the connections that make things work seamlessly and effectively. Think about the funnel you created for your specific business: users are essentially voting at every turn, saying yes, *I am willing to spend more time with you* (by reading content, saving items in a cart, etc.—all the actions that drive them to transact), or saying no. Truly delighting your end user as you move them through whatever actions you want them to take is tough, so don't take those no votes personally, but do pay attention to them!

FIGURE 6. 1: WHERE TO PUT THE PAYWALL?

TOO SOON AND YOU'VE LOST THE USER; YOU HAVEN'T HAD A CHANCE TO CONVINCE
THEM OF THE VALUE OF THE PRODUCT. TOO LATE AND THEY'VE ALREADY GOTTEN
EVERYTHING THEY NEED. LEAN ON YOUR UX DESIGNER TO FIND THE SWEET SPOT.

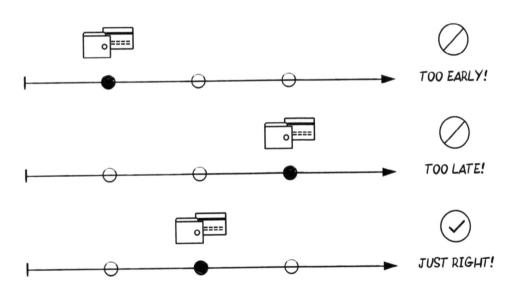

TOO EARLY!

TOO LATE!

JUST RIGHT!

THE ONLY ONE

ON WHAT

DOESN'T IS

WHO VOTES

WORKS AND WHAT

THE USER.

FIGURE 6. 2: WHAT'S NEXT?

THE FUTURE OF YOUR PRODUCT DEPENDS ON ITS RECEPTION.

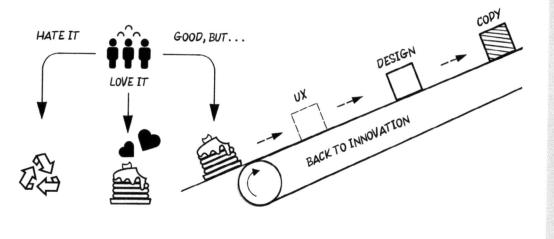

SCRAP

Most of your hypotheses didn't pan out

It takes guts to scrap. But it's smart, cost-effective, and it allows you to redeploy resources into other initiatives. You don't want to blow your entire budget knowing that there are better opportunities out there. And even though you're letting go of an idea in its current iteration, you may be able to repurpose elements of it. Whatever happens, in your next endeavor you'll be starting with insights, lessons learned, and hypotheses disproven—all viable outcomes.

LOOP

Roughly speaking, half of your hypotheses panned out

Look at what went well, how you failed fast, and create a plan to course-correct. You may want to loop back to valuable consumer insights, change paper stimuli, alter prototype or MVP material, or refine your end-user cohort. What tweaks are necessary to go back through the steps in such a way that it will lead to a product with a better chance of adoption?

MOVE FORWARD

Majority of your hypotheses are correct

Once you've delighted your consumer, it's simply time to get into market. Your team is aligned and you have clear marching orders for your developers. You've answered all the critical unknowns, and you're feeling confident about metric performance and the odds of success.

"THE ONLY REAL MISTAKE IS THE ONE FROM WHICH WE LEARN NOTHING."

— HENRY FORD

Ford's greatest achievement was finding ways to lower the cost of the automobile in order to make it accessible to middle-class Americans while still paying his workers a fair wage.

SUPPORT YOUR DECISION

Whether you're scrapping, looping back, or moving forward, be prepared to provide succinct reasons to support your decision. This is where metrics matter because they translate into facts—especially since empirical data tends to have greater weight for those who aren't entrenched in the project. Communicate your ideas clearly as those you're presenting to likely have little time to spare.

Now that you have a growing base of information, pull out your **Tip the Scale** information. Are the experiments helping you reduce your unknowns? Which hypothesis is performing better and how do the metrics from your experiments support this? Are you discarding or revisiting your **What Ifs**? You can return to the project of estimating the size of your opportunity, and, with more data, you can create a more accurate picture of the marketplace. But don't lose sight of the most important task, which is delighting your end user and determining whether you're solving an unmet need.

DON'T LEAVE THE LEARN STAGE UNTIL YOU'VE CONVINCED YOURSELF THAT YOUR DATA TELLS AN ACCURATE STORY.

MIND–SET

DISCE

ERNING

EVERYBODY THINKS
IS BEAUTIFUL.
DIDN'T, AND

THEIR BABY

BUT ROSEMARY

SHE WAS RIGHT.

CHECKLIST—

☑ Are you feeling confident in the instruments you're using? Be critical, question your own research, and consider looking at the problem from a different angle.

☑ Do you have the right arguments to decide to scrap, loop, or move forward?

☑ If you have more to learn, are you continuing to do rapid, bite-sized experiments? If yes, that's how you can iterate on questions as opposed to asking the "perfect" question.

☑ Are you seeing results from your experiments that have scale potential?

☑ Are you reducing your unknowns with everything you're learning?

☑ Are you staying with the findings whether the information confirms or denies your hypotheses?

☑ Are you able to easily convert data into lessons learned?

01.

Validate or prove
your assumptions
right or wrong

___

02.

Constantly refer
back to hypotheses
and your knowns
and unknowns

___

03.

If you're ready to scrap,
think about the time
and headaches you
saved yourself

___

KEY
TAKEAWAYS

04.

If you're looping back,
have confidence that
you learned what you
needed to learn

05.

If you're moving
forward, be fast
and decisive

Want to see our process in action?
Visit InnovatorsAnonymous.com/Case-Studies

ACT

MAKE YOUR
MOVE

STEP

07

LEAD THE WAY

This is where leadership styles count the most, because what you need is clear and concise communication about what's working well and what is less understood. It takes skill to shape a message that balances the risk a leadership team has to endure in the dangerous game of inventing new lines of business or starting a business from scratch.

The good news: you have much of the information you need to present your results. Using your assessment and original financial model, show whether you've shifted from your original set of assumptions, and if so, how. Explain what you can now claim as **Knowns** and be courageous enough to lay out what you still don't know. Use your **What If** scenarios to counterbalance the **Unknowns** and demonstrate your "good / better / best" predictions. You can even integrate the results from your experiments to show how you have avoided **Vanity Metrics**.

TRUE LEADERSHIP MEANS THINKING BEYOND YOUR OWN NEEDS TO THE GREATER GOOD OF THE BUSINESS.

BE REAL

Good leadership is not showmanship. It's not using fancy testimonials, factoids, or visual aides to present an inaccurate picture of where you are. Even if you don't see that you've fallen prey to this approach, others will; get a second and third opinion to hold fast to objectivity. A simple presentation style will help you demonstrate your willingness to be candid as you explain whether or not the initiative was a success. Success and failure are not binary—there are likely parts of your product or service you feel confident about and others you feel less confident about, and it's important to present the full picture.

Let us step back a bit. By this point you've been in development and you're gearing up to release your MVP, which means your stakeholders are likely dealing with some level of fatigue as well as business pressures that will make them want you to deliver faster no matter your pace. As with anything else, there is always a thirst for more. So how do you avoid this friction? By staying aligned: clearly agreeing to business goals and your road map to achieve them, touching base periodically, including all pertinent stakeholders, and addressing issues as they arise. The fact is that you have an obligation to delight not only your end user but also your funders. Listening is vital to understanding the mind-set of your investors so that you can internalize their concerns. In some ways, the hardest part of building a new business is winning the confidence game—with honest, collaborative communication. So whether you have good news or bad news, make it a winning proposition.

"I HAVE NOT FAILED. I'VE JUST FOUND 10,000 WAYS THAT WON'T WORK."

— THOMAS EDISON

By bringing mass production and teamwork to the process of innovation, Edison, who held over 1,000 US patents, laid the foundation for industrial research laboratories.

CELEBRATE

Take a bow for not falling for the **Stupid Money** trick. You and your team have spent your dollars wisely in many ways: not leaping into development for a poorly tested concept, delaying expensive marketing and communication plans, staying under the radar, and assessing whether to loop or move forward. If you've decided to scrap, know that it's not an embarrassing moment—this kind of clarity and courage is what builds careers.

KEEP AT IT

It's likely you'll need more end-to-end business experiments to move from high-engagement product work to market-adoption testing, and the same is true for scaling your product or service. Good leaders will support you and your team through this maturation process because great innovation takes many forms; sometimes you are innovating around internal operations, while other times you're innovating around pricing and customer-service or customer-experience enhancements for a product that has already proven itself. As you move from **MVP** to **VDVP** in sprint releases, it's important to think about the full scope of operationalizing your product or service. Every stage of business growth requires patience, commitment, and speed. (A tricky combination, we know!)

For better or worse, the work is never done; the pressures on your product could change, and it's likely that there are more product iterations in your future as you respond to customer feedback and fluctuations at large. Constant changes in technology, competitive landscape, and geopolitical climate are factors that influence outcomes for businesses. The good news is that people have more patience for products that are truly evolving.

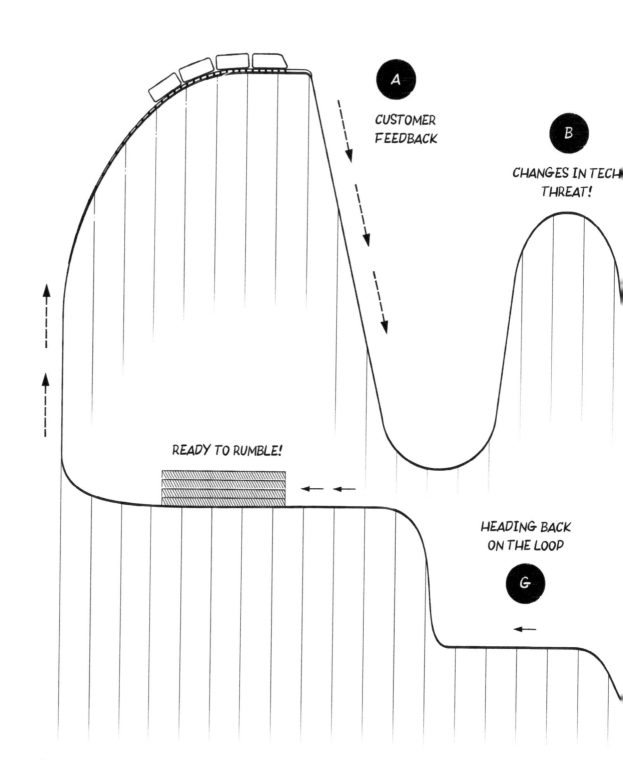

A

CUSTOMER FEEDBACK

B

CHANGES IN TECH THREAT!

READY TO RUMBLE!

HEADING BACK ON THE LOOP

G

FIGURE 7. 1: THE ROLLERCOASTER RIDE OF INNOVATION

THERE IS RARELY A STRAIGHT LINE TO A NEW PRODUCT. INSTEAD, IT'S AN ADVENTURE WITH TWISTS, TURNS, AND SURPRISES. THAT'S PART OF THE JOY AND THE CHALLENGE OF THE PROCESS.

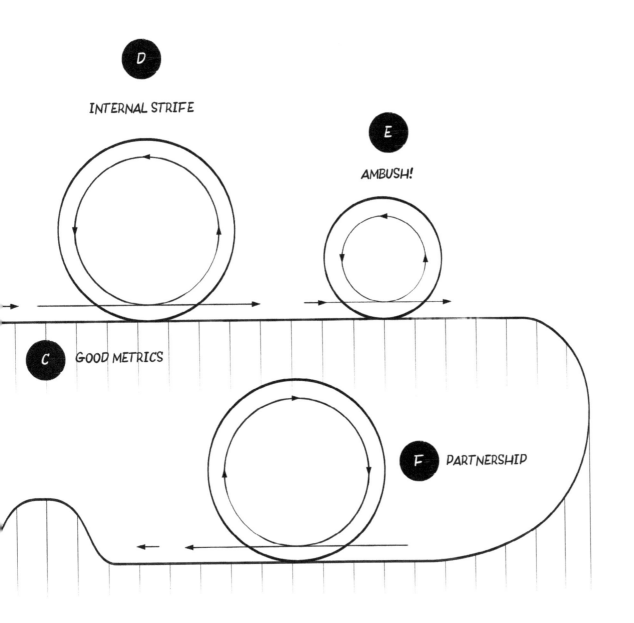

DESIGN

MIND-SET

CHECKLIST—

◯ Have you mapped out the rounds of funding you need to continue to develop this business opportunity?

◯ Have you revisited your financial model to focus on the right baseline case? Is that informed by what you've learned from **What Ifs** and **Knowns?**

◯ Have you created your product road map to move from **MVP** to **VDVP?**

◯ If you're using a transaction model, do you envision a freemium model or an immediate "commit wall"?

◯ How do you plan to test **Willingness to Pay (WTP)** to price your product?

◯ What new product experiments do you need to do to allow your digital product to mature?

◯ Have you had a transparent conversation with your leadership peers? Do you have board buy-in?

- ✓ Are you conceiving or refining your marketing funnel? Considering how users arrive, sign in, sign up, engage, and return to your experience?

- ✓ What dependencies do you have on distribution channels?

- ✓ Do you have an overall operational plan that encompasses the end-to-end business? What new cycles of innovation do you need to support?

- ✓ Are you staying aligned with your stakeholders? Have you been communicating with them along the way?

01.

Focus on your
leadership skills

_____

02.

Communicate facts
and figures honestly
and clearly

_____

03.

Carefully plot your next
budget round

_____

KEY TAKEAWAYS

04.

Engage in stealth
mode as you move
toward VDVP to ensure
a strong public launch

___

05.

Layer in scalable business
processes and back office
operations once VDVP is
in sight

___

Want to see our process in action?
Visit InnovatorsAnonymous.com/Case-Studies

CLOSE

"Take what you like and leave the rest" is something you hear in other anonymous support groups, and we think it applies here, too. Taking part in *Innovators Anonymous* means applying our process to your circumstances to see what works and what doesn't. We think it's useful advice no matter the environment.

Why? Because we live in a constant state of newness; culture pushes technology, and technology allows culture to express itself. This back and forth is where technology gets its meaning—from its ongoing interaction with culture, which we see as the birthplace of creativity. And we believe that technology is at its best when it responds to the world at large, when its creators wonder, "What is our culture asking for? How can technology meet that need?"

The process we've created is our attempt to help technology be at its best, to find a way to wonder aloud and create something that the world is waiting for. Conceiving of this process, we originally thought that there were eight steps, but as we worked out the kinks, we realized there were actually seven. There was no way we were going to stick with eight simply because that's where we began; we adapted with the material. In essence, we are human and this process is entirely human—that's the beauty and the crux of it.

When it comes to selling your creation, the hard truth is that no one can offer a fail-safe path to market. Yet this process is incredibly cost-effective—by not building too soon, by keeping your focus in the right place at the right time, by letting go of a product iteration that isn't performing, you get to learn and refine. For those of us who are in this for the long haul, "learn and refine" is the name of the game.

What one skill drives the entire process? Listening. Specifically, listening to the cacophony of influences and using what you're learning to drive the process forward. Easy to say and hard to do. Which is why we offer you these steps as a guide. Come back to them as you need.

The truth is innovation is not for the faint of heart. What we know is that trying to minimize risk and wanting something right away are twin desires that can be at odds; think of the adage "fast, cheap, and good—choose two." Yet minimization of risk happens as you continue to iterate. How do you get there? By asking the right questions, seeing things as they are, letting go of fear, and being agile—as a team. The process doesn't have to take very long and it can even be fun (spoiler alert!). For instance, one of us may or may not have fallen asleep during a marathon Google hangout, and yes, that's our idea of fun.

Let us acknowledge a simple fact: it takes courage to create. But if courage is what gets you into this mess, harmony is what gets you through it. Finding the customer-centric "there there" everyone is looking for is what makes it all worth it—the courage, the harmony and even the mess.

As you work through this and meet with success or failure, let us know how it's going. Because when you're in the process you're a part of the process, too.

ACKNOWLEDGEMENTS

■

We are fortunate to be surrounded by a fantastic pool of talent—culled from the people we have had the pleasure of working with over the years. Like us they know the process of innovation backwards and forwards. This book was very much a collaboration and we would like to take this moment to thank everyone who made it possible, specifically:

Erika Anderson, who is not only a writer but also an interpreter, helping us to organize our thoughts while simultaneously capturing our sentiment, and presenting it all with humor, elegance, and clarity.

Ricardo Portocarrero, whose beautiful designs and diagrams make complex concepts easy to absorb. The look and feel keeps the book from being boring, which is no easy feat.

Patrick Thompson, for intimately understanding our title, and capturing the human emotions behind it with his movie poster-worthy illustration for our book's cover.

Hope Gunston, whose ability to highlight the big picture while also catching any details helped us stay on the straight and narrow. She's lived the process so many times that she was able to make sure the content reflected reality.

Leslie Matis, whose excellent project-managing skills kept the wheels turning on this project and, more importantly, on our client assignments so that we could focus our time.

Albert Tien, who helped us understand the real value of the book early on with his extensive knowledge of how to get past pain points when it comes to user experience.

Jimmy Rau, for being our toughest critic on all matters, including in his field of expertise, design. With his amazing sense of objectivity, he helped us stick to simple truths. And he created the book website.

Katie Webb, who brought her detective skills to the fore in researching images and quotes. Her organizational skills kept everything in line, and her efforts on social media garnered interest in our book.

Darius Zagrean and Andrew Greenstein at SF App Works, who have helped shape and validate the seven steps over the years by outputting phenomenal code every single sprint. They even won the London hackathon!

Our families and friends, who have offered us the utmost patience as we dedicated weekends to the book, and read successive drafts. Know that your responses really did shape our thinking!

#IA

INNOVATORS ANONYMOUS.COM

CPSIA information can be obtained
at www.ICGtesting.com
Printed in the USA
FSHW01n1410080618
49064FS